Lincolnshire
COUNTY COUNCIL

COMMUNITIES, CULTURAL SERVICES
and ADULT EDUCATION
**This book should be returned on or before
the last date shown below.**

OSK

25. AUG 10	2 2 JUN 2009	0 5 DEC 2009

To renew or order library books please telephone 01522 782010
or visit www.lincolnshire.gov.uk
You will require a Personal Identification Number.
Ask any member of staff for this.

EC. 199 (LIBS): RS/L5/19

D0542945

Other books from Macmillan

Why Otters Don't Wear Socks
Poems by Roger Stevens

The Dog Ate My Bus Pass
Poems chosen by Nick Toczek and Andrew Fusek Peters

Red Lorry, Yellow Lorry
Poems chosen by Fiona Walters

The Monster That Ate The Universe

Poems by

Roger Stevens

Illustrated by Jane Eccles

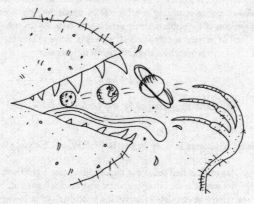

MACMILLAN CHILDREN'S BOOKS

For Ruby

With thanks to Ricky Jo Boom and Rubber Rhino
for the title track.

First published 2004 by Macmillan Children's Books
a division of Macmillan Publishers Limited
20 New Wharf Road, London N1 9RR
Basingstoke and Oxford
www.panmacmillan.com

Associated companies throughout the world

ISBN: 978-0-330-41523-1

3 5 7 9 8 6 4

A CIP catalogue record for this book is available from
the British Library.

Printed and bound in Great Britain by Mackays of Chatham plc, Kent

Contents

Get Your Poems Here

Roll up, roll up
Get your poems here
They're lovely

Four verses a fiver
Can't say fairer than that
Couplets – a pound a pair
Free metaphor with every purchase
And I'm cutting my nose off to spite my face

Roll up, roll up
Get your poems here
They're lovely

Bespoke ballads
Made-to-measure quatrains
Genuine haiku
Guaranteed all the way from Japan
Written on the slopes of Kilimanjaro
Seventeen P a syllable
That's seventeen times seventeen . . .
Tell you what
Call it three quid
And I'll throw in two extra syllables

Roll up, roll up
Get your poems here
They're lovely

Poems sublime
Poems that rhyme
And rap poems
Don't forget we gift-wrap
And we gift-wrap rap
All poems ready to take away

Roll up, roll up
Get your poems here
They're lovely

Free Roger McGough with every sale

Haiku

When I write haiku
I always seem to have one
syllable left o

ver

Hallowe'en

Darren's got a pumpkin
Hollowed out a treat
He put it in the window
It scared half the street

I wish I had a pumpkin
But I've not and it's a shame
I've got a scary carrot
But it's not the same

A List of Words

Ready, get set,
When I give the word
Go!

Long words
Short words
Ambitious words
Dull words
Angry words
Alarming words
Quaint words
Charming words
Mmbled wrds
Mispronounced wards
Anagram sword
Crosswords
Bidly spalled words
Key words
Secret words
Three little words
Words for fridges
Made of magnets
In-your-ear words
(words) in brackets
Having words
And words to give
The word is out
The word is love

Snow

Snow falls in China

And the children are building

A fat snow Buddha

Chicken School

Period one – simple clucking

Period two – more clucking

Period three – clucking with attitude

Period four – clucking with indecision

Period five – pecking in dirt

Period six – pecking in gravel

Period seven – rhythmic and jerky neck movements

Period eight – clucking (revision)

Escape Plan

As I, Stegosaurus
stand motionless
in the museum
I am secretly planning
my escape

At noon
Tyrannosaurus Rex
will cause a diversion
by wheeling around the museum's high ceilings
and diving at the curators and museum staff
while I
quietly slip out of the fire exit
and melt
into the London crowds

Juggling Genes

I wonder if scientists
Could give me some new genes
Genes that will build me a super-strong body
That can lift wardrobes and run
As fast as a train
Some genes that will make my brain so clever
I can invent a giant machine that will solve
All the Earth's problems
And genes that will give me smaller ears
As mine, at the moment, tend to flap in the wind.

Please Note
(after William Carlos Williams)

Who has eaten
the plums
that were in
the fridge?

I was
going to take them
to school
for my break

Keep your
thieving hands off.
The bar of chocolate
is mine also.

Sonnet Number One

The moon doth shine as bright as in the day
I sit upon the see-saw wondering why
She left me. Boys and girls come out to play.
But I'm bereft. I think I'm going to cry.
I gave her chocolate and I praised her skill
At skateboarding and football not to mention
Wrestling. As we slowly climbed the hill
To fetch some water, did I sense a tension?
She seemed preoccupied. She hardly spoke
And as we turned the handle to the well
I asked her, Jill, please tell me it's a joke.
She said, I've found another bloke. I fell,
I rolled, head over heels into the dark
Down to the bottom where I broke my heart

Sonnet Number Two

Don't sit upon the wall, Mum said, you'll fall
As sure as eggs is eggs, and break into
A thousand shards of shell, and that's not all
You'll lose your albumen and yolk as well.

But did I listen? No, for I was young,
Thought I knew best. I wouldn't slip. No way.
I climbed up on the wall. Quite difficult.
(I had no arms or legs.) It took all day.

But there I sat at last. An onion whizzed
Right past my ear. A second and a third.
I lost my balance. Fell. All in a tizz.
Hit the yard – hard! Splattered.

And then I heard
A soldier say, Quick fetch the pan, I'm famished.
For supper we'll have omelette.

Spanish.

Dad, Don't Dance

Whatever you do, don't dance, Dad
Whatever you do, don't dance
Don't wave your arms
Like a crazy buffoon
Displaying your charms
By the light of the moon
Trying to romance
A lady baboon
Whatever you do, don't dance

When you try to dance
Your left leg retreats
And your right leg starts to advance
Whatever you do, don't dance, Dad.
Has a ferret crawled into your pants?
Or maybe a hill full of ants?
Don't Samba
Don't Rumba
You'll tumble
And stumble
Whatever you do, Dad, don't dance

Don't glide up the aisle with a trolley
Or twirl the girl on the till
You've been banned from dancing in Tesco's
Cos your Tango made everyone ill

Whatever you do, don't dance, Dad
Whatever you do, don't dance
Don't make that weird face
Like you ate a sour plum
Don't waggle your hips
And stick out your bum
But most of all – PLEASE –
Don't smooch with Mum!
Whatever the circumstance
Whatever you do –
Dad, don't dance

Who Says a Poem Always has to Rhyme?

There was a young man called Frank
Who kept his pocket money in the . . . *

When he'd saved enough he bought an electric viola
And celebrated with a can of co . . . **

When he plays the viola the whole house rocks
It makes your shoes dance and it frightens your . . . ***

Frank plays his viola all the time
Who says a poem always has to . . . ****

* Post Office
** -conut cordial
*** granny
**** have a similar sound at the end of the line as it
had at the end of the line before?

The Holding~Your~Breath Contest

We held a Hold-Your-Breath contest
Me, Sammy, Sean and Sid
Sid held his breath for a fortnight.
We're going to miss that kid

Crumbs

My first is in baker and also in bread
My second's in miller and also in bread
My third is in cake and also in bread
My fourth is in wrapper and also in bread
My last is in doughnut and also in bread

My whole thing is found
Near the mouth, more or less,
And you often find crumbs there.
What am I? Can you guess?

(Answer: a beard)

The Monster That Ate the Universe

I began with a pancake
But why stop there?
So I ate the spoon
And the table and chair

What's my name?
The Monster that ate the Universe

I ate all the cutlery
I ate the cheese grater
The cooker, the microwave
The refrigerator

What's my name?
The Monster that ate the Universe

I wolfed down the kitchen
The dining room, too
I slurped up the bathroom
Including the loo

What's my name?
The Monster that ate the Universe

I chewed up the house
I gulped it all down
I ate the whole street
Then I swallowed the town

What's my name?
The Monster that ate the Universe

I devoured the country
Then what do you think?
I drank the ocean
I needed a drink

What's my name?
The Monster that ate the Universe

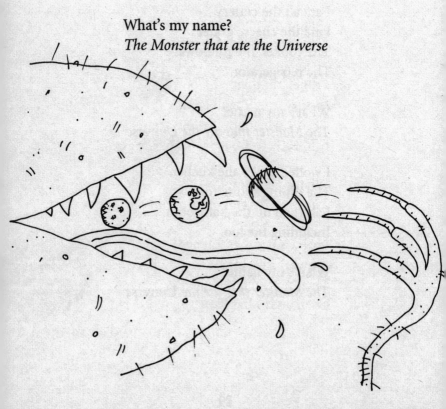

Then the Earth I consumed
The planets, the sun
I was still feeling peckish
And having such fun

What's my name?
The Monster that ate the Universe

So I gorged on the galaxy
Then the galaxy next door
I was still feeling hungry
So I gobbled up more

What's my name?
The Monster that ate the Universe

I dined on them all
As the prophets all feared
Then I swallowed myself
And (burp!) disappeared

What's my name?
The Monster that ate the Universe

In the quiet that followed
A little bird sang
Then nothing. Just silence.
Then a very big Bang!

Crack of Dawn

The sun is up
It's time to eat
So where are my providers?
Still in bed!
So I sit outside their door
And miaow very loudly
I'm sure they meant to
   get up at the crack of dawn
To feed me

When they've let me in
(after I've tugged at the carpet
under the door for a bit)
I jump on the bed and purr
And lick their faces
And, to communicate my desire for food,
(as if that were a lot to ask)
I chew the pot plants
And if that doesn't work
I eat the radiator

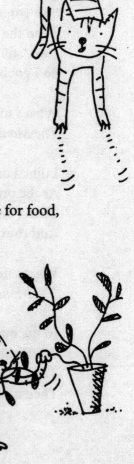

Okayku

Those less able Japanese scholars

Often wrote poems with exactly seventeen words

But they never became popular

Ghost School

The school building
Looks like any school building
Like your school building I expect
A little out of focus, maybe
A bit blurred round the edges

But the children seem vague
Slightly two-dimensional
They flicker
As though they are on a TV
With very poor reception

Sure, the children chatter and shriek
Like children do
But their voices sound distant
As though the volume control
Has been turned down
As though the treble control
Has been turned up

How I came to be here
In this strange school
I've no idea.
As I walk along the corridor
I can hear the children laughing
In the classroom
I can hear the teacher
Joking

But when I go in
Everyone falls silent
They stare at me
And run from the classroom
Screaming

Why are they so scared of me?
I haven't done anything

Best Holiday

We had our holiday at home this year
Dad bought two tons of sand
And dumped it in the garden
He hired a huge spotlight
And tied it to the guttering
So it looked like the sun was blazing down
Like in Spain

Then we put on our cossies
And sat in deck chairs
Listening to a tape of ocean waves
It was dead realistic

Dad painted a washing-up-powder box
With pound signs
And stuck a handle on it.
Then we kept pushing our money through the slot
Until it had all gone

Dad said the ice creams were a fiver
And Mum said we couldn't afford it
It was dead realistic

We paddled in a tin bath
Full of dirty water
We played beach tennis
And had the beach to ourselves

I cut my foot on a piece of glass
And had to go to hospital
For a jab
We pretended we couldn't speak the language
It was dead realistic

Next year Dad says
We might have an Italian holiday
In Mrs Pasolini's garden
She lives next door

Chutney

Sixteen jars

Of tomato chutney

Sit in the cupboard

Chuckling

The Poetry Grand National

The horses line up
They're under starter's orders
They're off

Adverb leaps gracefully over the first fence
Followed by Adjective
A sleek grey

Simile is overtaking on the outside
Like a pebble skimming the water

Halfway round the course
And Hyperbole is gaining on the leaders
Travelling at a million miles an hour

Adverb strides smoothly into first place

Haiku had good odds
But is far behind – and falls
At the last sylla-
ble

And as they flash past the winning post
The crowd is cheering
The winner is
Metaphor
Who quietly takes a bow

Items in the Edward Lear Museum

A runcible spoon and ticket (first class)
Thirty-nine bottles of Ring-Bo-Ree
A scarlet flannel, a crockery jar
A sieve that has travelled the Western Sea
Some oblong oysters (just their shells) and the hat
Of Mr Quangle Wangle Quee
And in pride of place, in a crumbobblious case
A branch from the old Bong Tree
Some waterproof clothes, the beard and a nose
And a branch of the old Bong Tree

The Superhero List

After accidentally rescuing planet Earth
I was offered the chance
To become a superhero.
Unfortunately all the best positions
Had gone.
This is what was left:

Liquid Refreshment Machine Repairman
(A lifesaver on a hot day)

Mosquito Man
  (Keeps insects at bay)
  Salting Icy Roads Man
  (Saving skidding lorries and cars)
  Confectionery Dispenser Unit Man
  (Saving melting chocolate bars)
   Tadpole man
      (Rescuing frogs from logs)
      Stick Insect Man
        (rescuing stick insects
          from frogs)

Ten Pence Down the Back of the Sofa Man
(Where only the bravest superheroes go)
And, of course, Supergran
(but I don't somehow think so)
I could have been Captain Decisive
But I couldn't make up my mind
I could have been Captain King of the Hill
But I didn't feel so inclined
I could have been Captain Upholsterer
But I'd never have recovered
I could have been Captain Apathy
But I couldn't be bothered

And I Went

And I went
I don't even know
What you're talking about
And she went
You being funny?
And I went
Is anyone laughing?
What's your problem?
And she went
You looking for a fight?
And I went
Is there one here then?
And she went
You looking at me?
And I went
And she went
And I went
And she went
So I went.

The Origin of the Clerihew

Edmund Clerihew Bentley's fame grew
When he invented the clerihew
But if he'd wanted a fortune he would have been wiser
Inventing the double cheeseburger, with fries, Sir

The Museum Says

Be awed as you climb my heavy
stone steps built to last
I am old by your standards
Two hundred years have rolled past
But young by the measure
of all of the treasure I hold
My tomes tell of kingdoms long gone
in vast rooms of old gold
My pillars of marble reach up
to the cold, winter sky
And my heart is of granite
A dinosaur sleeping am I

The Art Gallery Says

Hey, I'm cool.
My lines sweep. Zoom.
Catch the eye.
They turn beneath
a fresh spring sky.
Groovy textiles.
Razzamatazz.
This year's black.
I'm now.
Hip.
Jazz.
My wood is polished.
I have awkward seats.
Ergonomic.
White walls with crazy
coloured paintings.
Manic
I am a bird about to rise
into the clouds.
Organic.

Freedom

Below me you are fast asleep
But I am out of sight
As I crawl across your ceiling
A black shape in the night

I am heading for the window
Where the moon lights up the sky
No more a small, cramped tank of glass
My eight arms wave
    Goodbye
    Goodbye
    Goodbye
    Goodbye
    Goodbye
    Goodbye
    Goodbye
    So long . . .

Grandpa's Will

Dear Family, now I'm dead
And gone to my rest
Here's what I've left
For those I love best

For Tony, my son
And Sandra, his wife
My referee's whistle
And old army knife

For Bernard, my grandson
I've left my TV
He obviously loved it
More than he loved me

For Danni, his sister
Who visited twice
This photo of me growing old
Should suffice

Dear Hattie, who nursed me
Gets my one-bedroomed flat
And ten thousand pounds
Goes to Jeffrey, my cat

The School for Nice Children Who Are Always Top of the Class

Nine o'clock
How to whisper, cough, giggle
And drop marbles in assembly

Nine-twenty
How to race along corridor

Nine-twenty-five
Maths – how to muddle up number blocks
And forget five times table

Ten o'clock
English – how to forget capital letters
And full stops

Ten-forty-five
How to drop litter in playground
And kick ball on to roof

Eleven o'clock
How to talk in line
And answer teacher back

One minute past eleven
How to fidget
Outside Head's office

Two minutes past eleven
How to be sullen and rude

Three minutes past eleven
How to stand in school entrance
Waiting for Mum
Who has been called away from work

How to have regrets

Chalk

As we walk across this hill of chalk
It's hard to imagine
That once these hills
Were below the sea
Chalk is the sediment
Left by a million tiny creatures
On the seabed
I think of that
As we walk upon this thin skin
Of earth and grass
Beneath the blue sky
And a burning sun

Mayfly's Diary

Monday October 1st

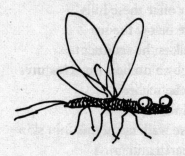

The sun's coming up
I'm born
I'm alive
Look at the grass
The sun
The sky
Made a new friend
Together we fly
Sun's going down
Must go
Goodbye

Laser Eye

Mum said, Baby Kevin
Has a laser eye
I guess that means
He has X-ray vision
And when he's older
Will be able to project a beam
Of light that cuts metal
From his eye
And he'll rescue people
Trapped in cars
And if he's attracted to the dark side
Of the force
He'll be a worthy foe
For James Bond

Then Mum said,
No, I said a *lazy* eye
Which is disappointing really
In fact
The exact opposite

On a Poet's Day Off

On a poet's day off
Haikus can have a couple of
Extra syllables

On a poet's day off
Moons rhyme with July
And never wane or wax

On a poet's day off
Clouds blow across the sky
Daffodils grow in clumps
The breeze doesn't sigh

On a poet's day off
Words take wing
And similes can have a rest
Like
As not

On a poet's day off
There's no such thing

Gherkin Car

I am the Picasso of Poetry
Ear nose blue pink eye spoon
Burnt ochre
Sienna
Five walnuts
Vienna
A six-year-old child could write this
Exclamation mark
Wonky

Donkey

Teachers

Teachers are happy
All of the while
Teachers are cheery
Teachers all smile
Teachers have eyes
In the backs of their heads
Teachers remember
The good things you said
Teachers are friendly
Teachers are kind
Teachers can always
See into your mind
Teachers will help
If you're stuck with your sums
Teachers like stillness
But not wriggle-bums
Teachers are visitors
From Outer Space
Teachers play Scrabble
But never kiss chase
Teachers like writing
Their writing is neat
Teachers are honest
Teachers don't cheat
Teachers walk or ride bikes
(They don't have much choice

They can't afford cars
And they'd love a Rolls-Royce)
Teachers eat salad
And stinky cheese
Teachers have patches on jackets
And knees
Teachers are fair
Though they can give cross looks
Teachers have hobbies
And they love marking books
I want to be a teacher
When I leave school
Or else a Rock Star
Which is equally cool

List of Lists

I love making lists so much
I've made a list of lists

Shopping list
Things-to-do-today list
List of best friends whose shoulders you can cry on
Top-ten list of fast food shops
List of gruesome punishments
List of favourite excuses
List of favourite bands on *Top of the Pops*
List of ingredients for giant pizza
List of wishes in case a magic genie appears
List of favourite words that rhyme
Sir Bobby Robson and Sir Alex Ferguson (List of knights)
Bewildered. Shell-shocked. Confused. (List of daze)
List of presents wanted at Christmas time
List of things to do tomorrow
And number one on tomorrow's list is . . . ?
Make a new list

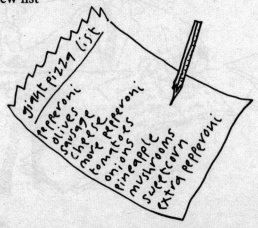

Introducing Dad

If I may, Miss
I'd like to introduce my dad
Mum left us last year
And that made him really sad
He thinks you're rather pretty
And his favourite colour's beige
And it isn't that uncommon
To date women half your age
And we all know that he's bald
Beneath that funny flick of hair
You just have to humour him
And pretend his hair's all there
His feet smell a bit funny
And his brain's a trifle slow
And you haven't got a boyfriend, Miss
So . . . could you please give Dad a go?

Wonderful Pupil

It's lovely to meet you at last
Mrs Dracula
    Your son is a wonderful pupil

He's very good at science
Especially the study of blood

He did a beautiful drawing in art
Of a bat

And he was top in geography
He's very knowledgeable
About Transylvania, isn't he?

You and Mr Dracula
Must be very proud.

Where is Mr Dracula?
Oh, he'll be along later
When it gets dark

Jolly good
I'm looking forward
To meeting him

Beetle in France Haiku

A large black beetle

Crash-lands on the cool floor tiles

And wonders, What now?

Flower

We were pleasantly surprised
When Clint from 6B
Turned into a flower.
Sara said,
Doesn't Clint smell nice?
Aziz said,
Shall we pick him and put him in a vase?
Tara said,
We could press him and put him in a book.
Teacher said,
Who'd have thought it,
A rhododendron, too.
How delightful.

Seabed Romance

The romance between
The hermit crabs
Is not going too well
They are both so shy and retiring

They won't come out of their shells

Cousin

This summer

A distant cousin came to stay

But I didn't see him

He was too far away

I Wandered Lonely
(In the style of William Wordsworth)

I wandered lonely as a snail
Who leaves a trail o'er leaf and stick
When all at once I saw a thrush
Who smashed my shell against a brick

Farewell

If the final farewell
Could have been planned
You would have said,
'I'll miss you. Please don't go.'

You would have held her hand
One final time.
You would have tried
To unfound her fears.

Instead Mum gets a phone call
And you walk into the garden all alone
To watch the blur of butterflies
Through tears

Parents' Evening

Hello, Mrs Spinner
Now, about your son, Sam

First of all I must say
I'm sorry to hear about your Rottweiler
Sam says it's been poorly
Well, the number of times it's eaten Sam's homework
I'm not surprised
And then it gave Sam dog flu and he was away
On the day that Brighton played Spurs in the cup
And it was a shame that he chewed Sam's PE kit
What's that?
You don't have a Rottweiler?
How strange

By the way, Mrs Spinner
May I congratulate your husband
On being chosen to represent England
in the next Olympics
You must be very proud
He's a shot-putter, Sam says
And Sammy tells me you're the model
In those bra commercials

What's that?
You have to be going?
You have something to say to Sammy?
Well, lovely to meet you at last
Tell Sammy I'm looking forward
To seeing him tomorrow

Goodbye, Mrs Spinner
Goodbye

The Ancient Mariner

It is an ancient mariner
And he stoppeth one of three –
He stopped the person just in front
Why didn't he stop me?

I wonder *why* he stopped him –
Had he a tale to tell?
About a long and wondrous voyage
Into the depths of hell?

More probably a story
About a trip to Wapping
And how he bought his gran a card
And where he did her shopping

But it's as well I was not stopped
By that sailor, sad and smelly
Because I have to hurry home
There's football on the telly

Six Eggs

Six eggs
Hide in their dark
Cocoons
Nursing
Sunshine

Top Scorer

Give me the ball
And I always score
I'm a first-class striker
That's for sure

I missed it that time
But the wind was wrong
And those new balls
I've said all along

They don't kick right
And I've bruised my shin
Otherwise
The ball would have gone in

So pass me the ball
Next time I'll score
I'm a first-class striker
That's for sure

Our New Teacher

Last Christmas our teacher went skiing
Leaping from glaciers with glee
She zoomed down ravines like a champion
But she couldn't get on with 6B

At Easter she sailed around Iceland
Pitting her wits 'gainst the sea
She rode the huge waves single-handed
But she couldn't get on with 6B

In summer she went pony-trekking
Through the wild mountain ranges of Chile
Went white-water rafting in a tiny canoe
But she couldn't get on with 6B

Now 6B have left for the big school
And teacher has us in her charge
And we love to hear of her adventures
And we're all well behaved – by and large

So we asked, Do you miss your old class, Miss?
And she went all quiet and sad
Then her face lit up and she started to laugh.
What me? Miss 6B? Are you mad?

Best Friend

When my best friend died
Nothing anyone said
Helped much
And I cried and cried
And cried and cried

I'll tell you something.
We did everything together
Both caught colds
Caught measles, caught frogs
Got caught scrumping

We were both football crazy.
I was Beckham, he was Shearer
I'd cross the ball
He'd score the goal
Now the referee has sent him off

My best friend
Was the best holiday you ever had
Where the sun always shone
The holiday you never wanted to end
And then it did

Extract from a Shepherd's Diary

A long time ago in Bethlehem, December 23rd

It's freezing up here on the hill
Nothing to do
But gaze up at the stars
Once the sheep have all been fed

Tonight's my last night
Then back to the day shift, thank God.
Tomorrow night
I'll be tucked up warm in bed

A Footballer's Prayer

Dear God
Please bless my feet
May they kick the ball
'real sweet!'
Keep my balance
Keep me on my toes
Help my teammates
Outfox my foes
May my feet
March to victory
Win the match and the double
And may my feet always
Walk away from trouble

Teachers' Playtime

It's wonderful being on duty
When the teachers come out to play
See them running and shouting and leaping about
On a sunny winter's day

But I have to send Mr Walton
Back to the class for his coat
And Miss Atkins's stayed in – there's a spot on her chin
(Her mother gave her a note)

Mrs Bateman hits Mr Fitton
She says he has stolen her ball
So I give her a lecture on sharing and caring
And I make her stand in the hall

Mrs Peck falls over and twists her foot
She limps, but there's nothing to see
So I ask her to zoom to the staffroom
To fetch me a cup of tea

Mr Owen is scared of Miss Pryor
He's hiding in the boys' bog
He says he'll stay there all day if she won't go away
Cos she's trying to give him a snog

Mrs Rowlands, who works in the office,
Does a handstand against the wall
You can see her navy-blue knickers
It's not very nice at all

I love it on playground duty
Bossing teachers still gives me a thrill
So I ring the bell two minutes early
And . . .

Mr Walton . . .

STAND STILL!

Grandma's Jigsaw Puzzle

Grandma wanted
To find the house
She lived in as a child
Long ago
At the beginning of time
When the grass was greener
When the light was brighter
When sound was sharper
And a pound
Was worth twenty shillings

Dad took us
Round factories
And schools
And new houses
Where there were once fields
And we gazed at brick walls
Trying to piece together clues
And Grandma said, It was so long ago
Everything's different now

And in the end
The jigsaw puzzle
In Grandma's head
Was too difficult to solve

Trick or Treat

As we lurch along the darkened street
This spooky Hallowe'en
Freddy is dressed as Frankenstein
His face a sickly green
Darren is dressed as a mummy
Bandaged from head to feet
Sarah is a scary ghost
Wrapped up in a sheet
I am dressed as Dracula
My cape is red and black
But I wish I knew who the zombie was
Creeping along at the back

Heart

If you stood upon the moon

What would you see?

Rearrange my heart

And that is what you mean to me

Spell to
Make Mum Smile

Say, Good morning Mum

You look particularly

pretty. How about

A nice cup of tea?

When Dad
Went into Space

What was it like in space, Dad?
You've seen the snaps, he said.
Like being in a giant church
Or rising from the dead

The colours were much brighter
Louder and somehow scented
To tell you properly I'd need words
That haven't been invented

How's it feel to be back, I asked
Dad smiled and shed a tear
The gravity – well, that's a drag
But I love the atmosphere

Rocket

Last year
Dad planted rocket in the garden
For the salad

It grew as normal until
One night, without warning
It launched itself into the sky

Whoooooooosh, it went
And exploded in a ball
Of blinding yellow and cream dressing
K E R B L A M

That, said Dad
Is rocket science

Forming a Band

I said,
Let's form a band, OK?
My mate said great –
But what shall we play?
How about Punk?
Boogie-woogie? Hip-hop?
Acid-soul-house-jazz or Pop?
60s, Flower-power, Disco, Soul?
70s influenced? Plain Rock 'n' Roll?
Ambient-psycho-techno-thrash?
Heavy metal? Hard core? Slash?
80s, Romantics, Garage . . . Shed?

I replied, Let's play
With my skateboard instead

How to Find Our House

Head south until you reach the end of land
Take off your shoes and socks
Walk on to the beach
And down to the ocean
Across the sand and rocks

Listen to the whoosh of surf
The suck of shingle
The sea's wet kiss
Turn left
And head for those distant cliffs
In the mist

You'll pass the tangle of orange-glow netting
Snagged with pebbles and shells
Pass the bleached beached driftwood
And the rotting-crab smells
Pass the broken plastic chair
Thrown back by the waves
Pass the black, cracked truck mudguard
And the message on the sand
Jesus Saves

When you reach the Martello Tower
Turn left, with your back to the sea
And in the window of that white cottage
The one on the left
There's me
Writing this poem
And waving.
You're just in time for tea.

Why the Bat
Flies at Night

Once, when the moon was as bright as the sun
And the stars lit up the sky
And the day and the night were both as one
The bat came flying by

The bat flew by fast and furious
And attached to his back with string
Was a basket. The animals were curious
They said, Bat, what is that thing?

Ah, said the bat, well, this afternoon
I was given a task to do
To take this basket up to the moon
But what's in it? I haven't a clue.

But the bat was no long-distance flyer
And he had to lie down to sleep
So, due to the others' insistence,
The lion opened the basket to peep

Then all at once from the basket
There came a most terrible sight
A shadow that fell like a dark net
Bringing the blackness of night

And that is why bats rise at twilight
And they sleep through the bright hours of day
Why they chivvy and chase the dark slivers of night
The darkness they let get away

Why Otters Don't Wear Socks

Poems by
Roger Stevens

This collection contains laughs (including chuckles, guffaws and grins); sad moments (some); thrills (many); rhymes; haikus; rude words; adjectives (assorted); made-up words (including wham-wig); nonsense and a fat penguin called Pete.

Farewell, Pete

I had a little dinosaur
Nothing would it eat
But a chocolate cupcake
And my best mate, Pete

Red Lorry, Yellow Lorry

chosen by **Fiona Waters**

from Stairway to the Clouds

I took a stairway to the clouds
and a camel to the moon
a trampoline to Timbuktu
and a rocket to my room.

I've travelled many places
in many different styles
near and far and deep and wide
millions of miles.

But no matter how I wander
no matter where I roam
of all these special journeys
the best one is . . . back home.

Paul Cookson

A selected list of poetry titles available from Macmillan Children's Books

The prices shown below are correct at the time of going to press. However, Macmillan Publishers reserves the right to show new retail prices on covers, which may differ from those previously advertised.

Why Otters Don't Wear Socks   978-0-330-44851-2   £3.99

Poems by Roger Stevens

The Dog Ate My Buspass   978-0-330-41800-3   £3.99

Poems chosen by Nick Toczek and Andrew Fusek Peters

Red Lorry, Yellow Lorry   978-0-330-44338-8   £3.99

Poems chosen by Fiona Waters

Monster Poems   978-0-330-42048-8   £3.99

Chosen by Brian Moses

All Pan Macmillan titles can be ordered from our website, www.panmacmillan.com, or from your local bookshop and are also available by post from:

Bookpost, PO Box 29, Douglas, Isle of Man IM99 1BQ
Credit cards accepted. For details:
Telephone: 01624 677237
Fax: 01624 670923
Email: bookshop@enterprise.net
www.bookpost.co.uk

Free postage and packing in the United Kingdom